STANLEY

Other I CAN READ BOOKS® by Syd Hoff

Danny and the Dinosaur

Julius

Sammy the Seal

Oliver

Who Will Be My Friends?

Albert the Albatross

Chester

Little Chief

Grizzwold

The Horse in Harry's Room

Thunderhoof

Barkley

Santa's Moose

Barney's Horse

Mrs. Brice's Mice

An I Can Read Book®

STANLEY

Story and Pictures by

Syd Hoff

HarperTrophy
A Division of HarperCollins*Publishers*

HarperCollins®, 📖®, and I Can Read Book® are trademarks of HarperCollins Publishers I▮

Library of Congress Cataloging-in-Publication Data
Hoff, Syd, date
  Stanley / by Syd Hoff.
      p.   cm. — (An I can read book)
  Summary: Chased away by the other cavemen because he is different,
Stanley finds a new and better way of living.
  ISBN 0-06-444010-9 (pbk.)
  [1. Man, Prehistoric—Fiction.   2. Self-confidence—Fiction.]
I. Title.   II. Series.
PZ7.H672Ss   1992   91-12266
[E]—dc20   CIP
                                                                AC

New Harper Trophy edition, 1992.

STANLEY

A long time ago there were no houses
and people lived in caves.

Stanley lived in a cave,

but he did not like it.

10

The cave was cold.

So Stanley was cold.

His head hurt because

he had to sleep with it on a rock.

Bats flew around as though
they owned the place.

"Why can't we find
a better way to live?"
asked Stanley.

14

"This is good enough for us,"

said the other cavemen.

"Why isn't it good enough for you?"

The cavemen carried clubs.

They were very tough.

Stanley was tough, too.

But he liked to plant seeds

in the ground

and watch them grow.

18

He liked to paint pictures.

He liked to be nice to people.

He was kind to animals.

The other cavemen did not want Stanley to act this way. "Can't you act more like a caveman?" they asked.

Stanley did not answer.

He went on planting seeds

and painting pictures.

He went on being kind to animals
and nice to people.

He even started saying things like

"Please," and "Thank you,"

and "Lovely day today, isn't it?"

This made the other cavemen
very angry.

"You can't live here," they said.
"Beat it!"

They threw rocks at Stanley
and chased him away.

"We're sorry you lost your cave,"
said the animals.

"I don't care," said Stanley.

"It was cold anyway."

28

He looked for a place to live.

"You can't live in a nest,"

said the birds.

"You can't live in the water,"
said the fish.

"You can't live in the ground,"
said a worm.

"Maybe I can live in a tree,"
said Stanley.

"Not while I'm up here,"

said an ape.

"Maybe I can live in space,"

said Stanley.

He jumped off a rock.

34

"Ouch!" said Stanley.

"I can't live in space!"

35

Stanley saw a field.

"Does anybody mind if I live here?"

he asked.

"I don't mind if you don't snore,"

said an animal

who was going to sleep.

"I don't mind if you don't

eat too much grass,"

said an animal who was eating.

"I don't mind
if you don't take up
too much room,"
said a very,
very big animal.

Stanley made himself at home.

"This is not bad," he said.

But suddenly the wind blew

and Stanley was cold.

The rain fell and he was wet.

"This is worse than the cave,"

said Stanley.

He made walls

to keep out the wind.

He made a roof

to keep out the rain.

He made a door,

windows and chimney.

He made a house!

"That's the first house I ever saw,"
said a field mouse.

"It's the first one I ever made,"

said Stanley.

"Won't you stay here

and live with me?"

"I can't. I belong in the field.
But I will come and visit you
from time to time,"
said the field mouse.

Stanley painted pictures.

He planted seeds in the ground

and watched them grow.

He loved his house.

But he was lonesome.

"I wonder how my friends are,"
he said.

The cavemen were out
hunting for animals.
They carried their clubs.

"Look who's after us

with their silly clubs,"

said the animals.

"Let's chase them out of here!"

They chased the cavemen.

Stanley saw the cavemen running.

"Don't be afraid," he said.

"I won't let them hurt you."

He made the animals go away.

"You saved us, Stanley,"

said the cavemen.

"Thank you."

"Come back and live in our cave,"
said one caveman.

"Caves are old-fashioned," said Stanley

"Come and see where I live."

He showed them his house.

"A cave is for bears.

A house is for people,"

said Stanley.

"You are right, Stanley,"

said the cavemen.

"This is the way we want to live."

They all made houses.

Stanley showed them

how to paint pictures

and plant seeds.

He showed them

how to be nice to each other

and kind to animals,

and everybody was happy.